How Ordinary Russians Clobbered Communism

An Insider's View

Lincoln Landis
Lieutenant Colonel, U.S. Army, retired

HERITAGE BOOKS
2014

HERITAGE BOOKS

AN IMPRINT OF HERITAGE BOOKS, INC.

Books, CDs, and more—Worldwide

For our listing of thousands of titles see our website
at
www.HeritageBooks.com

Published 2014 by
HERITAGE BOOKS, INC.
Publishing Division
5810 Ruatan Street
Berwyn Heights, Md. 20740

International Standard Book Numbers
Paperbound: 978-0-7884-5560-5
Clothbound: 978-0-7884-9030-9

Foreword

The title of this book "How Ordinary Russians Clobbered Communism" refers to the recent Cold War that ended in a whimper. Dr. James H. Billington, Librarian of Congress, spoke these words to describe "the collapse" of the Soviet Union in 1991:

> *We are living in the midst of a great historical drama that we did not expect, do not understand, and cannot even name.* -- Address to American Academy of Arts and Sciences.

Dr. Billington re-enforced his stark assessment some 20 years later, declaring: *implosion of the Soviet system was totally unanticipated, and we still don't understand it.* (Russia House, August 26, 2011.)

From my own experience in U.S.-Russian liaison during key periods of the Cold War, I would offer a simpler explanation: communism in the Soviet Union began to collapse the moment Premier Joseph Stalin brought the U.S.S.R. into the United Nations in 1945.

This fateful act of diplomacy, in my view, opened Soviet communism to the scrutiny of my one-on-one, U.S. liaison activity during such key periods as the Berlin Airlift crisis 1948, the Berlin Wall crisis 1961, and the détente period beginning in the 1970s.

The author

Contents

Illustrations follow pages 23 and 42.

I. Cold War turning congenial 1945-1946

A "congenial war" brings into view a perspective gained from patterns of liaison activity "in the trenches of the Cold War." The description of warfare as congenial in nature unfolds through unraveling experiences in four periods: the Cold War turning congenial 1945-1946; unraveling during the Berlin Airlift crisis 1947-1948; unraveling during the Berlin Wall crisis 1961-1963; and unraveling during détente 1976-1977.

The decade of the 1940s led me in unexpected, yet rewarding, directions. World War II started off with a prospect of intimate wartime involvement, while a subsequent military career lodged me in an unfamiliar kind of warfare -- a standoff against our once-ally the Soviet Union! The Red Army in Occupied Germany suddenly became a new enemy plunging this young second lieutenant into the trenches of a seemingly endless Cold War.

Yet, my outlook broadened as I became a grassroots *eyewitness* to an array of congenial Russians. The circumstances that appeared before me emerged during the military occupation of Germany by the United States and the Soviet Union from 1945 to 1991 and created the notion that a "congenial war" would become a more appropriate term than a "Cold War."

This idea grew from my observations that the Russians with whom I had dealings throughout my liaison-oriented career did not suggest hostility but rather resembled, in most instances, reasonable people living under the constraints of a totalitarian system. While the cosmopolitan view of "the Cold War" indicated a hostile engagement, at my level the liaison activity defined itself as a peaceful engagement. Thus, I am strongly persuaded to write about "a *congenial* war," not a *hostile* "cold war."

Upon receiving our West Point diplomas in June 1945, we brand-new "shave-tails" were assigned to training camps in preparation for assignment during the active war still raging

1

against Japan, and as new second lieutenants, we were seemingly destined for an invasion of that country. Those of us who had volunteered for the infantry proceeded to Fort Benning, Georgia to undergo a program that was expected to focus upon getting ashore on the island of Honshu, possibly by the end of the year.

Such plans quickly disappeared after President Truman's decision to drop the atomic bombs in August 1945, and many of us in the combat branches headed for occupation duty in Germany. We infantry officers seemed to be facing a future of boring static duties: training exercises with little realistic purpose -- over and over again.

The "Cold War," however, would change all of that because we had not expected, in cadet training, to view the Soviet Union as a potential enemy. After shipping out from New York harbor in October, I had no reason to expect a direct confrontation with Red Army occupation troops in Germany, a scenario that, of course, had not been a part of West Point's curriculum.

We arrived in France, where our group congregated outside of Paris at Camp L'Etemps and heard General Allen, a seasoned combat commander, who gave us an inspiring talk. The general was interested in our young careers and advised us to understand "these are the days of the empire," cautioning that American officers must not abuse the authority suddenly conferred upon them. He stressed our obligation to show respect for the devastated German people, with whom we would have daily contact. The general also hadn't anticipated a standoff with Russia, our World War II ally that had paid a heavy price in helping America defeat Hitler's armies.

With General Allen's wise counsel in mind, we moved out to undertake new troop assignments. I arrived in the German State of Hesse, in the northern-most portion of the American Zone and proceeded down a winding cobblestone road into the desolate, U.S.-Russian border area. Russian and British Occupation Zones were just a few hundred yards to the east and north, respectively.

My assigned unit was the combat-weary, highly-decorated Third Infantry Division that had fought through Anzio in Italy and southern France. What an honor for us green second lieutenants of the Regular Army! The "big picture" for me was also impressive with my new responsibility: manning guard posts on the Russian zonal border that were manned against border troops of the KGB.

At this time, the Red Army was not considered an explicit threat. Yet, by the Yalta Agreement of January 1945, armed guards of the United States, Britain and Russia were placed in a "no-man's land." This desolate area existed between the American and British occupation zones on the west and the Russian zone on the east, close enough "to take potshots" at one-another. Might such an environment lead to armed conflict between these three occupying powers? Apparently higher headquarters in Heidelberg hadn't given such conditions any amount of serious thought.

The American zonal border where my soldiers confronted Russian guard posts followed a historic trace between two German States, "our" Hesse in the West and "the Russians'" Thuringia in the East. For the first time, the terms "west" and "east" would be capitalized to indicate the growing strains between the western allies and the Russians in the east. The landscape was wide-open, with no barriers separating the two sides and a mere string of opposing guard posts marking the separation of terrain between the Seventh U.S. Army and the Soviet Eighth Guards Army. Suddenly, had not Lincoln Landis, a Hoosier fresh out of West Point, by a stroke of luck, become a key military figure in post-war Germany?

The soldiers on duty in the guard posts along the zonal border were on the lookout for Russian soldiers who might be wandering into the U.S. Zone. The same rules seemed to apply to Russian guard posts on the other side of the border -- to control the passage of wayward Americans who might enter the zone of Soviet responsibility.

I gained the duty of guarding the northern-most border section of the American Zone where the British, Russian and American Zones of Germany intersected, an auspicious piece of territory with lingering political, military, and strategic significance. My authority over this region seemed to be immense and, for a new second lieutenant, a full measure of pride. Suddenly, I had received authority of a degree not even imagined by General Allen. What if the folks back in Logansport, Indiana had an inkling of my newly-acquired status!

In a thoughtful vein, I began to sense that the United States had become woefully unprepared for occupational responsibilities following the end of World War II. My duties fell to me without benefit of detailed consideration and guidance emanating from higher headquarters. Support of the status quo and reporting anything that changed it became my self-generated priorities. My decisions with regard to border incursions or violations had better be sound for the sake of the US military and for the United States!

At this time, it seemed apparent that Americans at all levels did not know whether the Russians were friends or enemies, although the hope remained strong that they would be friends. On this point, I often wondered what reasonable purpose could be served by initiating hostilities between allies after they had jointly gained a huge victory over Germany and Italy. Yet, I had no reason to feel assured that the future would be one of cooperation and trust that had marked most of the allied military effort against the common enemy, Germany and Italy.

One example of confused attitudes regarding America's relationship with the Soviet Union filtered down to troop-level when two Russian lieutenants ventured by motorcycle through one of my guard posts and suddenly appeared at my office several miles removed from the border. After, as a newly-named company commander, I recovered from amazement in seeing them at my headquarters, I asked them: "Why did you drive through my guard post? My guards ought to have shot at you to prevent you from coming here."

Their response was a relaxed shrug, while the three of us proceeded in broken German to reach a measure of

4

comprehension. The unexpected foreign visitors said they were on a mission to request sulfa drugs for treating their soldiers' venereal disease. (At the time, I wondered if they might be more concerned about their own health problems rather than the VD status of their troops.)

In order to respond to their query, I quickly phoned higher headquarters to obtain official guidance, explaining that the Red Army officers were standing in my presence. The colonel on the other end of the phone reacted swiftly: "My God, are you kidding me? How can you possibly say that Russians are in the American zone and actually standing in your office?"

I calmed him down by assuring him that there was no Soviet invasion of our area, but that two Russian lieutenants had arrived with a request for sulfa drugs for their troops' venereal disease. As the colonel began to accept the fact that there was no imminent danger of military aggression, he responded with an emphatic "No, we have no sulfa drugs that we can provide to them."

I put down the phone and reported to my extraordinary guests: "I'm very sorry, but we do not have sulfa drugs to share with you." With that, they smiled broadly, acknowledging that this American lieutenant had made an effort to accommodate their request, and handed me two bottles of wine. They saluted, did an "about-face," jumped on their motorcycle, and disappeared as quickly as they had arrived. Fortunately, my soldiers on the guard post allowed them to cross the border without creating an international incident even before the "cold war" had begun.

That was the last that I would see of these lieutenants or other Russian military personnel during the balance of my duties on this section of the U.S.-Soviet border. On reflection, I wondered whether other Russian troops held such a positive attitude toward America in the face of typical propaganda they were receiving on a daily basis. I was ready to give them "the benefit of doubt" and to believe optimistically that peace and cooperation between the United States and the Soviet Union might come about in the foreseeable future.

These Russians were frank and friendly, giving me a very favorable impression of Russian troops and caused me to recognize their pro-American attitude and to consider that their communist indoctrination was beginning to unravel.

In a few months, I received orders stating that the Third Infantry Division was to be deactivated, and its colors would be returned to the United States. My next assignment was with an all-black engineer unit, of the bridge-building type, that was, like the Third Division, also highly-experienced in combat. Only the officers, in that period, were white, and it was my unusual good fortune to be the "only white guy" on our regimental basketball team. My official duty was as Regimental Mess Officer, and my chief assistant was Staff Sergeant Starks, who held a master's degree in music from Cincinnati. Working together, we were able to assist the down-trodden and hungry Germans who formed long lines to ladle our left-overs that we placed in 55-gallon drums for them.

My duties also included defense counsel of the regiment, followed several weeks later as trial judge advocate. After nine months, I volunteered for a special program and was re-assigned to study the Russian language in a six-month course at the European Command Intelligence School located at Oberammergau, Germany.

II. Unraveling during the Berlin Airlift crisis 1947-1948

During this training in the summer of 1947, the Truman Doctrine began to challenge communist efforts to subvert the governments of Greece and Turkey and to extend Soviet dominion in Eastern Europe. At last, I began to sense that "the humdrum nature of occupation duties" was fast disappearing in the face of an emerging Russian military threat in Germany. The Cold War was unmistakably coming into view in Washington D.C.

I was not surprised to learn, upon completion of language training, that I was assigned to a position requiring my newly-acquired linguistic skills. My higher headquarters now became the 7th U.S. Army, and I would be responsible for the northern half of the American Occupation Zonal border opposite the Russian Zone. At this time, the overall 7th Army wartime structure was being replaced by a more maneuverable force, the United States Constabulary. This new concept was better suited to guard the border between the American and Russian Occupation zones in order to thwart any possible invasion from the East. *I wondered whether such a military threat could be possible when Russian soldiers I had met showed friendliness rather than hostility.*

Upon my arrival at Constabulary Headquarters in Heidelberg in September 1947, I enquired about the nature of my new assignment in American-Russian Liaison. The Constabulary G-2 (Intelligence) officer, a lieutenant colonel, responded with an amused look on his face: "Just get up there on the border and liaise."

Later, I would realize that the colonel's cavalier manner was not one of indifference, but a reflection of his, and his headquarters' total lack of understanding of what was going on in the border region. I was shocked that our highest military headquarters in Occupied Germany didn't seem to "have a clue" about their existing relationship with the Soviet High Command at Weimar, Germany. I was also perplexed about what this liaison assignment would involve for an American second lieutenant of Infantry. In effect, it seemed that Constabulary Headquarters was sending me into "the vast unknown" and was not taking the post-war Occupation responsibility seriously.

Feeling eager to take on an interesting new challenge cloaked in a bit of mystery, I proceeded to Hersfeld in the German State of Hesse, a major town centrally-located in my assigned area of responsibility. This region comprised the northern half of the entire American-Russian zonal boundary. I was astounded to learn that I was replacing an officer, five military grades higher, a full colonel and that I would be responsible for the trace of the entire boundary between the German States of Hesse in the American Zone and Thuringia in the Russian Zone. This situation was, in my mind, ridiculous, but who was I to question my higher military authority!

The colonel who departed from this liaison position had also been responsible for the southern half of the American zonal border, between the States of Bavaria in the American Zone and Saxony in the Russian Zone, and his successor for this area was another second lieutenant Jim Ryan, with an office in Coburg, Bavaria. What was going on here? As the prospect of confrontation with the Soviet Union gradually seemed to be growing, official contact with the Soviet Eighth Guards Army in this critical military region was being turned over to the U.S. Army's youngest, least experienced officers! Again, this was a new concept of keeping U.S. Russian relations "on an even keel." The whole idea seemed that the United States had given no serious thought to the aftermath of Allied victory over Nazi Germany.

Of course, duty is duty, and there was no time to question how irresponsible was the emerging relationship with a possible military enemy! Besides, Jim Ryan and I shouldn't complain about having such huge responsibility placed on our shoulders. (Little did I realize that this liaison duty would prove to be the most exciting and rewarding of our military careers.)

I joined up with my liaison team, four soldier-interpreters of Ukrainian descent from western Pennsylvania: Sergeants Kluchanovich and Morosky and Corporals Trocki and Zavitsky. They were bright, young, well-trained soldiers who served also as drivers of my four assigned jeeps. It was immediately apparent that my team had a strong esprit and were supremely happy with the prestige of dealing directly with the Soviet Army of Occupation in Germany.

As team chief, I represented U.S. Constabulary Headquarters in Heidelberg to "maintain contact as needed" with my Red Army counterparts, Lieutenant Colonel Garber and Major Sazanov. These officers worked in tandem from their headquarters, Soviet Eighth Guards Army in Weimar, Thuringia in the Russian Occupation Zone. Again, the huge military gap between Lieutenant Landis sitting across the table from a Soviet team comprised of a lieutenant colonel and a major made no sense whatever. I was convinced that Garber and Sazanov had to be sending back to their headquarters the ridiculous nature of this lop-sided liaison situation.

Performing the liaison role, I was informed, meant that the American liaison team would enjoy diplomatic immunity and carry out its duties in military field uniform without personal weapons. Thus, the entire U.S.-Russian demarcation line in Germany became the direct responsibility of two, low-ranking second lieutenants, operating separately -- Landis in Hersfeld, Hesse, and Ryan in Coburg, Bavaria, and their Soviet counterparts were a much-higher-ranking, combined team of a lieutenant colonel and a major!

This duo of second lieutenants, Landis in the north with the key terrain feature, the Fulda Gap, and Ryan in the south (much less likely to hold military significance), both holding heavy responsibilities far exceeding their lowly military rank. It was natural that Landis and Ryan would grow to enjoy a strong fellowship, sharing the knowledge of their key positions if war should break out. Their duties were so "out-of-kilter" as to give way to the best of humor, bordering on hilarity. With zero involvement by Seventh Army Headquarters at Heidelberg in our work facing the powerful Soviet Eighth Guards Army in Weimar, we would soon learn to do a bit of scheming, sharing tactical tips on how to take subtle advantage, if needed, of our Soviet counterparts.

At the same time, we recognized that our newly-formed Constabulary Headquarters was "in the dark" about border matters and about the nature of the Russians with whom we worked. Because of this, our two-man association would become vital because we were morally supportive of one another, feeling that we alone, "two second johns," had "the best jobs in the world." The key reservation, of course, was that a Soviet invasion of the West, we hoped, would not occur "on our watch." In a few words: we had unimaginable duties, but with the potential for intriguing work to do with no supervision from higher headquarters!

Our unwritten, underlying duty was obvious: to keep our eyes and ears open for a possible military invasion by the Red Army. No regular reports were called for by Constabulary Headquarters, and here were two lieutenants remaining on-call, 24 hours a day, seven days a week. Of course, we remained obligated to pursue any and all instructions from Heidelberg, such as to contact the Russians as problems arose and to respond to queries presented to us by our Russian counterparts, Lieutenant Colonel Garber and Major Sazanov.

On the frivolous side, a young, highly-attractive and stylishly-dressed young lady appeared at my quarters in our assigned dwelling place, a Hersfeld hotel, seeking conversation and sociability. I was of course wary, while momentarily impressed by these unexpected circumstances, and my better judgement prevailed as I found it advisable to dispatch her, especially when she acknowledged having useful contacts in the Russian Zone.

Settling into the awesome duties of military liaison officer without the issuance of identifying documentation persuaded me to value highly the paint-job on the front bumpers of my jeeps: "Amerikanskaya-Russkaya Svyaz" (American-Russian Liaison) in black letters on a yellow background. As a feeling of confrontation between the United

10

States and the U.S.S.R. was becoming evident in 1947, these jeep bumpers were a hoped-for, legitimate statement of diplomatic immunity. They proved to be my liaison team's unorthodox, but vital, first line of defense against possible Soviet intimidation. In fact, their value, as will be seen later, became nil later on when a serious incident overrode their hoped-for diplomatic effectiveness.

Despite a growing sense of uncertainty about our team's perception of a looming "Russian threat," Constabulary Headquarters had little to say about a heightened level of danger emanating from the Russian Zone. Ryan and I were not comfortable with an American stance in 1947 which amounted to one of "wait and see" if the Russians would misbehave. In any event, the U.S. Army seemed to rely upon my liaison team's "catbird seat" on the zonal border to detect any aggressive military movement from the east. Yes, we thought – we might detect a threat, but our two small unarmed liaison teams could not deflect an invasion of Soviet tanks from the East!

In the period of a few weeks after my assignment at Hersfeld, I witnessed a first-hand sample indication of U.S.-Soviet relations following a phone call from the U.S. Constabulary guard post on the zonal border reporting that two Red Army officers had arrived on site and wished to meet with the American liaison officer.

I began to realize that the time might be ripe to test my skills of "liaising" as a military diplomat, while wondering what the Russians' extraordinary presence at the U.S. guard post at this time could mean. I proceeded with my driver Sergeant Pete Morosky to the border and approached the "visitors," who turned out to me Major Kris and Lieutenant Volkov from the Soviet guard post at Wartha, which would prove to be our established meeting place for U.S.-Russian liaison matters. Would this meeting perhaps signal a serious confrontation between Washington and Moscow?

To my surprised relief, Kris and Volkov were in an inebriated state, singing and swaying, arm-in-arm, in the middle of the road, singing Russian military scores in

11

discordant tones. On my previous meeting with Kris, the occasions had been of a military nature -- cordial and informal but, most certainly, without the presence of alcohol. On this occasion, however, the festive pair was distinctively out of character as they welcomed this serious and sober American liaison officer to join with them in a moment of unabashed drunkenness.

This climate of celebration seemed to be stretching my instructions from Constabulary Headquarters to "just get up there on the border and liaise." Nevertheless, as America's strategically-important military representative, I hunkered down and assumed the joyful spirit while declining Red Army proffers of booze. Soon I was swinging and swaying, arm-in-arm, between Kris and Volkov. The Russians were singing raucously a collection of Russian folk songs that, fortunately, included "Kalyinka," one of my limited repertoire of favorites from Russian language training. For 10 or 15 minutes, I produced my own gibberish in what must have resembled a comedic performance to our most-proper, Constabulary sentry, standing stiffly nearby. A strange trio we were – sloppily partying in "no-man's-land" of the desolate American-Soviet border region.

After a while, Major Kris got tired of singing and, assuming a most serious manner, turned to me while pointing to the Constabulary guard, a private soldier, who was in "spit-and-polish" uniform. "Look at your soldier," Kris said. "He is an aristocrat, just like you, but look at my hands, I am just a miner." I looked at them and, yes, it wasn't just dirty fingernails -- his hands looked tough.

Finally getting my bearings after the ridiculous songfest, I attempted to correct the Red Army major's inference that Americans were upper-class people. I responded: "No, he is no aristocrat; he is a private soldier. I too am not from an upper class, aristocratic family. I am like all the other lieutenants in the American Army. We are not wealthy. We are just ordinary citizens." Kris seemed puzzled and seemed to find my explanation hard to accept.

The major's humility and friendliness caused the American lieutenant to recall an earlier incident when, a year earlier, the two Russian lieutenants had crossed the border at their own risk to seek American sulfa drugs. They too had been respectful and appreciative although I had been unable to oblige them in their request. I recalled that they had thanked me, saluted smartly, and given me two bottles of wine before departing for the Russian Zone. The earlier pair of Russians and this pair impressed me that these were humane fellows in every meaning of the word.

I compared the earlier motorcyclists with Kris and Volkov in the friendliness I was now experiencing. "How could these soldiers be America's enemy?" I wondered while I weighed the alleged "Soviet threat" that was gaining prominence in the American Zone. These examples on the zonal border of Germany were good evidence that Russia remained America's ally, I thought. To me, suggestions of a "cold war" seemed to be grossly out-of-synch.

Then Major Kris became more serious and shifted to an emotional frame of mind. Still holding me arm-in-arm between himself and Lieutenant Volkov, he pleaded with me, with tears running down his face: "We must have peace with America. We must not have war between us." At this moment, Volkov chimed in, shouting: "We must have world peace!" With those words, he fired his pistol through his pants pocket, missing my foot by a few inches.

Visibly angered at his assistant's untimely misbehavior, Major Kris lost his patience and grabbed and berated his lieutenant. Meanwhile, as I was absorbing the good feelings exhibited by the major, I welcomed this turn of events because the joyful party over which I had no control, was coming to an end. I also soon appreciated the importance of the occasion that moved Major Kris to embark on this special celebration.

The date was November 7, 1947, and he and his lieutenant had good reason to drink and sing: the Thirtieth Anniversary of the Bolshevik Revolution. I valued being included in this unusual ceremony and agreed completely that there was nothing to be gained through going to war with one another. This example, in spite of Lieutenant Volkov's display of exuberance, seemed to indicate that the ordinary citizens of our two countries weren't far apart in their thoughts about peace and cooperation. *These Russians were frank and friendly, and it looked like communist indoctrination was beginning to unravel.*

Meanwhile, Constabulary Headquarters in Heidelberg continued to reflect its comfortable isolation from "the front lines" of a new Cold War during each of my visits to report my experiences. The Intelligence G-2 colonel always greeted "his liaising lieutenant" with an enthusiastic handshake and the same question: "Tell me. How are things out there? What's going on? What are the Russians like?" I responded simply that I had been "liaising" as instructed a few months earlier, and that things seemed to be under control with no sign of serious problems.

As the year drew to a close in December 1947, there seemed to be a growing concern at Constabulary Headquarters, when the Intelligence colonel sent my team a message suggesting the possibility of Soviet military aggression against the American Zone. He directed me to occupy a good observation point on New Years Eve in order to detect any Red Army movement westward through the "Fulda gap," a term that would become the focus of future U.S. defensive military actions.

This assignment meant that my driver and I would comprise an emergency, mobile outpost to observe whether the Red Army might launch a major assault against American troops at midnight of this special day. The presumption was that the Russians would select the precise moment when U.S. Forces would likely be in a state of festive celebration. In my positive relationship with Colonel Garber, Major Sazanov, Major Kris and, well, Lieutenant Volkov, World War III hardly seemed likely, but, perhaps, they knew something at higher headquarters that I didn't, and maybe it would be an interesting night.

Sergeant Morosky and I headed out to an appointed hilltop and settled in to await a possible military invasion! We used binoculars, gazing eastward and listening carefully for the typical sound of tank engines revving up in the distance. The night was clear, perhaps eerily so, and visibility was excellent. We waited and watched and listened, thinking that, in any event, this would be a most-remembered New Years Eve of our lives. It proved to be just that for me, although a raucous, exciting time, it was not.

Morosky and I waited until well past the stroke of midnight and observed absolutely nothing. In a way, it was quite a wonderful feeling. Then we hopped into the jeep and scooted on an uneventful trip back to Hersfeld. The pair were grateful at how the evening and early morning hours had panned out, realizing that, otherwise, they would be driving at breakneck speed westward, carrying the message: "The Russians are coming. World War III!"

My Russian liaison team found the coming year of 1948 to take on greater intensity. Public attention was fixed upon the communization of Czechoslovakia, with the defenestration of democratic leader Jan Masaryk. This sterner perception of the U.S.S.R. began to shred the earlier prevailing view that Western countries were uncertain whether the Red Army in Occupied Germany was a friendly or hostile force. At least among top decision-making layers in Washington, bilateral relations were probably becoming cold indeed.

Soon, my team also began to question its optimism about a happy future because Premier Stalin was showing signs of hostility. When the Soviet Union proceeded to blockade Western land access to West Berlin, he was taking a step to jettison his United Nations obligations. Consequently, a shift in Constabulary Headquarters' "supreme isolation" was not long in coming. This escalating standoff between East and West placed President Truman in a bind. How would the United States react?

Possessing a demonstrated nuclear warfare capability after the attacks on Hiroshima and Nagasaki in 1945, the United States enjoyed a military edge over the Soviet Union that did not have the bomb or the means to deliver it. Still, an armed escort of Western convoys to West Berlin appeared inadvisable at the time. Yet, some kind of effective action would tend to affirm U.S. leadership of the Western world against a growing communist threat. Finally, President Truman chose a non-provocative, military-technological, and ingenious course: the establishment, along with the British, of an air bridge to bring needed food and fuel supplies to West Berlin. He had decided against military action to break the land blockade that might have moved the two countries closer to World War III.

The Allied plan to thwart the land blockade via such a Berlin Airlift would utilize the approved air corridors from the Western Occupation Zones to West Berlin. One corridor extended from the British Zone, and two provided flights from the American Zone beginning at Wiesbaden and Frankfurt/Main enroute to Tempelhof Airbase in West Berlin.

The latter route had special meaning for my liaison team because it happened to provide flights directly above its regular meeting place at the Russian border guard post at Wartha. These flights proceeded to occur day and night at intervals of a few minutes and would possibly provide interesting background effects for liaison visits we would make to my "Bolshevik Anniversary friend" Major Kris. It would also provide an interesting and perhaps provocative touch during negotiating sessions on border matters that I might conduct with Colonel Garber and Major Sazanov.

On another occasion that summer, I happened to seek a visit with Major Kris at his Wartha border office with no official agenda in mind and was met at the border post by a Russian private on guard duty. His bedraggled uniform contrasted sharply with the U.S. Constabulary sentinel a few weeks earlier, when Kris referred to Americans as "aristocrats." On this occasion, with the Berlin Airlift well underway, Kris' guard bore a surly gaze, as if he wanted to have nothing to do with me.

Since the Russian private was reluctant to acknowledge my presence, I tried "to break the ice" by offering him a Lucky Strike cigarette. I got his attention, but he quickly rebuffed me, saying in Russian: "I like Russian cigarettes much better." With that, he tore a piece of dirty newspaper on the ground, loaded it with majorka from his shirt pocket, and started to light it. I quickly struck a match for him, and he took a puff as if it was "the best smoke in the world."

After a few minutes, we heard a roar in the sky from the West, and we both recognized one of our Berlin Airlift planes flying in the air corridor above. As it came into view, the private suddenly thrust his hand into the air with glee and hollered the only English word he probably knew: "C-forty seven!" His enchantment with seeing the American plane, even though the Airlift was a major irritant to the Russian hierarchy, paved the way for good communication between us. He quickly escorted me to Major Kris' office, where the major and I proceeded to have a casual meeting.

Remaining in my thoughts was the abrupt change of attitude by the border guard, from hostility to friendliness. I had noticed this process on numerous occasions, when a veneer of antagonism would give way to a readiness to be cordial and cooperative. I could not avoid the conclusion that a typical feature of citizens of this totalitarian society was that of a "split personality." *This was another indication that communist indoctrination was beginning to unravel.*

On another visit to Wartha, I introduced Sergeant Morris, a newly-assigned member of my liaison team, to Colonel Garber, who quickly asked in Russian: "You're Jewish aren't you?" Morris replied that he was indeed, and Colonel Garber added that he too was Jewish. Sergeant Morris then added that he had been born in Ukraine.

Garber responded: "I also am from Ukraine. What was your home town?" When Morris replied: "Kremenchug," Colonel Garber shouted: "That's where I am from as well." In a climactic moment, the Colonel asked Morris' age, and the sergeant replied: "51." With that, Garber grabbed Morris saying: "My God, so am I, and we went to school together!"

This Russian colonel was frank and friendly. Communist ideology was unraveling.

It seemed that "the Cold War" was taking on new meaning when, on another visit to Major Kris, the KGB suddenly arrived. It was a casual social call, when Sergeant Morosky and I were able to get past the Wartha border guard easily. During the chat with Kris, the back door of his office swung open, and two men in civilian clothes strode in without knocking. One of them, glaring at Morosky and me, spoke sharply to Kris in Russian, asking: "What the hell are the Americans doing here?"

Major Kris quickly countered: "Lieutenant Landis, the American Liaison Officer, and his driver, Sergeant Morosky are talking with me about border matters." The Russian visitor continued: "You know you are not supposed to have conversations with the Americans." Then, as if to reconsider what he had been saying, he asked: "Do they understand Russian?" and Kris replied pointedly: "Yes they do, and they understand what you have said."

The two visitors turned and slinked out the door, leaving Major Kris to apologize to us, adding with a shrug: "Lousy NKVD-sti!" (Soviet plain-clothes KGB secret police). This interchange placed a damper on our meeting, and we said "good bye," surmising that our good Major Kris could be in a heap of trouble. *Major Kris was frank and friendly. His commitment to communist authority was unraveling.*

Our solid relationship with Kris indeed proved to be short-lived. On my next visit to Wartha, in my new 1948 Chevrolet sedan, Kris was missing, and a comical-looking Russian official in a plain, blue uniform, lacking in insignia, appeared in his place. When I introduced myself, the official smiled stupidly, and refused to give his name or rank. After he started to light a cigarette, I waved his hand away and led him to come over to see my automobile.

The first words he uttered were: "You are just kidding. That is not your automobile." I opened the passenger door and pushed in the cigarette lighter. When it popped out, the Russian was confused and muttered suspiciously: "What's going on here?" When I gave him a light, he was delighted and said: "Kak originalny!" When I asked him repeatedly what had happened to Major Kris, he grinned softly and said nothing. I never saw Major Kris again, and this colorless, little man in a strange uniform had suddenly replaced him.

The fact that, now as a first lieutenant, I represented the American side as a very junior officer, the contrast with the rank of my counterparts had always been impossible to explain. Since I had replaced Colonel Frazier, the Russian tandem of Lieutenant Colonel Garber with Major Sazanov had finally become a matter for serious discussion. The Russians expressed their concern saying, in a diplomatic way, that the lack of balance in rank made the Soviet side feel uncomfortable. While they had full justification to speak out on this matter, they assured me that it was simply a problem of rank, and that they had no problem in dealing with me. *Lieutenant Colonel Garber and Major Sazanov were frank and friendly, and communist indoctrination was unraveling.*

I got the message and, wondering if I might be losing my authority and job that I truly valued, reported the Russians' frank statement of discomfort to Constabulary Headquarters. In a few weeks, an elderly-looking full colonel arrived to be a supervisor over my northern half of the Russian zonal border and Jim Ryan's southern half of the border. Fortunately, Ryan and I agreed that the colonel showed little interest or competence for the work and spoke no Russian. He established an office further back in the American Zone and made only an occasional appearance with me or Jim to see the Russians.

When Morosky and I took the new colonel out to meet Colonel Garber and Major Sazanov, he showed a lack of diplomatic skills by offering the Soviet officers a drink from his own whisky bottle. They responded with an acerbic comment: "No thanks, we don't drink on duty."

With the Berlin Airlift well underway in August, the existence of the Frankfurt-Tempelhof corridor seemed to be a reminder that it was located not only over my meeting place with the Russians at Wartha, but also of greater importance, over the "Fulda Gap." This geographic location between higher ground on the north and south began to gain significance on the American side as the most likely avenue for Soviet tanks if the Russians should choose to invade the West.

Meanwhile, routine events took place that required my liaison team's attention such as a requirement to return a Soviet soldier who wandered into the American Zone, perhaps in pursuit of a West German damsel, or in an effort to desert his military unit. In either case, I was directed, under terms of the recent General Clay-Marshal Sokolovsky Agreement, to return him to Soviet control.

Realizing that the soldier would rebel if he realized he was being returned to the Red Army, Morosky and I tied him firmly in the front seat of the jeep. This was a rare occasion when I was authorized to carry a pistol, and the soldier, upon realizing that he was being transported in an eastward direction, begged me to shoot him.

He placed his hand on his temple and asked me: "Please give me one little bullet right here." I managed to turn him over to Soviet authority at the Wartha guard post, and the soldier was quickly led away. We departed with strong concern about the likelihood that the soldier would be badly treated and probably executed without delay.

A most unusual task in "liaising" came to my team with a directive "to paint the border." Since there was no clear demarcation on the ground between the American and Russian zones, inadvertent crossings were possible by individuals bold enough to approach the border region as in the case of Americans who hunted for wild boar, a popular pastime for American servicemen on duty in Occupied Germany.

In addition, the possibility existed that American soldiers might inadvertently cross the border while hunting in the woods, or perhaps go into the Russian Zone in pursuit of East German female companionship. The Constabulary Headquarters directive also had in mind a need for American military aircraft patrolling the border area to be assisted in their navigation efforts by an opportunity to see clear markers on paved roads that would indicate the location of the zonal border.

With sparse guidance in mind as to "how to paint this piece of landscape," my team proceeded with paint sprayers, using orange and white colors. We painted the large stone markers that were placed many years ago at 50-meter intervals on the line delineating the boundary between the German States of Thuringia on the Russian side and Hesse on the American side. Through the woods my liaison team went, placing circles of alternate colors at shoulder height on trees selected because they were somewhat visible from one painted tree to another.

This was not a precise science, but the team did the best it could, trying meticulously to remain within the American Zone in accordance with the map's designation of the boundary line. Lightening the task, team members would occasionally observe a Red Army soldier peeking around trees in the Russian Zone. Presumably, the soldiers had cause to wonder what kind of foolishness the Americans were up to as the liaison team made its way through densely-wooded areas. In the middle of black-top roads, the team painted a large orange-and-white square to accommodate Constabulary pilots "flying the border".

A more eventful task lay before the team when Constabulary Headquarters asked me to explore a meadow for a special purpose on the American side of the zonal border opposite the village of Asbach in the Russian Zone. It seemed that American military personnel, with whom I was not familiar, had been close to the border east of the American town of Bad Sooden-Allendorf and had apparently left some material that ought to be recovered.

Not knowing just what material was meant, Morosky and I set out with two West German border police, whose purpose was to make sure that liaison team members did not by chance walk on the Soviet side of the border. As was customary, we Americans were not armed, but the German police carried pistols. As the team walked through the meadow with eyes cast downward, I suddenly realized that a

Soviet captain was leading a squad of soldiers, fully-armed, from Asbach in the direction of my team.

The captain crossed into the American Zone, which happened to be well-designated in that area, pointed his pistol at me, cocked the trigger, and ordered "rooky verkh" (hands up!). I of course complied, ordering my colleagues to do likewise, and told the captain in Russian: "I am the American-Russian Liaison Officer and have diplomatic immunity."

I was too occupied at this moment to charge that the captain was illegally entering the American Zone, because I felt compelled to calm down the German border police, who appeared ready to use their pistols. They seemed prepared to go into armed action against a squad of Red Army soldiers who had surrounded the team in a large circle, with rifles pointing at our group of four and were pressing all of us into the center. I used my rudimentary knowledge of German by declaring to the West German: "is goot, is goot," and it worked.

Then, under the captain's order, Morosky and I and the two border policemen followed him, hands raised, prisoner-style, across the border into the East German village of Asbach. I glanced to the rear, hoping that someone might be observing the incident and saw a German woman, a half-mile away gathering potatoes.

I thought correctly that no one had observed the arrest and, for a moment, wondered if we would ever survive to inform Constabulary Headquarters of our fate. Morosky and I were led to a nearby military headquarters building, where we were ordered to display military identification. Then we were brought outside the building to the place where the Soviet captain was standing.

At this moment, I observed that a Soviet soldier was having difficulty trying to drive my liaison team's jeep, with bumper emblazoned: "Amerikanskaya-Russkaya Svyaz" ("American-Russian Liaison,") that had failed to bring us diplomatic immunity. Noting that he was "stripping the gears" as he tried to drive it from the American Zone into Asbach, I became oblivious for the moment to my status as a prisoner. I turned to the captain and said in no uncertain terms, with translation assistance from Pete Morosky: "You will have to pay for my jeep if you don't let my own sergeant drive it."

As I had stepped out of character as a prisoner, it became the Soviet captain's turn to seemingly forget that he was in charge. The captain, whose name Morosov was similar to Pete's name, responded with a sheepish look as he motioned angrily to Morosky to go to his jeep and drive it. Pete did just that, taking good care of the transmission as he drove over rough ground from the American Zone into the Russian Zone at Asbach.

At this time, again disregarding my inferior status as a Cold War P.O.W. (and subordinate in military rank), I decided to build upon my previous success by issuing another order to the Soviet captain. With Morosky interpreting, I instructed Captain Morosov to take good care of the West German policemen and to be sure that they would retain their pistols upon return to the American Zone. Captain Morosov said nothing but appeared to take my advice seriously, as he had done concerning the stripped gears of the jeep. *He wasn't friendly but was straightforward. For the moment, my sergeant and I sensed that communist authority was unraveling in the dirty little East German village of Asbach.*

Next, the captain ordered his sergeant to get into the narrow back seat of the closed-in, jeep, managing to squirm in beside his sergeant. Again, it seemed that roles were reversed, and the American prisoners were in charge. Sergeant Morosky kept his role as the driver, and Lieutenant Landis assumed the commander's place up front in the passenger seat.

Off Morosky drove on the captain's signal from his scrunched position in the back. Morosky and I quickly realized that our exalted position was not reassuring because the Soviet sergeant was holding a tommy gun in his lap, and our jeep, with liaison markings on the front bumper, was heading in an unfavorable direction: *eastward* toward the Red Army rear area. *In spite of our immediate situation, communist authority looked like it was unraveling.*

Still, what a remarkable turn-of-events! The armed Soviet captain, on duty in the Russian Zone, had seemed confused about his absolute authority over a pair of uppity, unarmed American captives. Could it be that, down deep, he thought he might not be doing the right thing? *Or did he, like other Russians I had occasion to meet, have good feelings about Americans at the expense of communist ideology?*

This extraordinary jeep trip traveled over curvy roads a distance of several miles to a town, where Sergeant Morosky on orders of Captain Morosov, parked at a Red Army headquarters building. We Americans were led inside, where a group of young Soviet officers were having a meeting. They rose to their feet, appearing surprised at the arrival of Americans in military uniform, possibly the first they had ever seen. I thought that the Russians appeared anything but belligerent -- might they have been wondering if Pete Morosky and I might have been the advance element of an American invasion of the Russian Zone?

At any rate, our captivity continued in the absence of Captain Morosov and the presence of another captain, a headquarters officer-in-charge, who chose not to give his name. He seemed unprepared for our arrival but quickly stated that we were going to be processed further to the rear of the Russian Zone.

I protested in Russian, with some linguistic help from Morosky, that we were wrongfully arrested while performing our unstated liaison duties inside the American Zone – that we possessed diplomatic immunity and should be released at once. The captain ignored my statement in both words and body language. To break a moment of uncomfortable silence, I asked to use a telephone in order to call my counterpart Colonel Garber or Major Sazanov at Eighth Guards Army Headquarters in Weimar.

The captain scoffed and rejected this request, adding that it was impossible because such telephone numbers were not available. With this good opportunity to show some initiative that favored us prisoners, I was able to respond: "I

PRISONERS OF THE COLD WAR:
The Village of Asbach Remembers

Over a half-century ago, we of the Class of 1945 sensed that the war against Germany and Japan might be won without our help. At the same time, we could not know that we would be the first West Point class to embark upon a new kind of war—the long struggle against communism. Such were my thoughts in the summer of 1993, when I found the opportunity to revisit the tiny village of Asbach, Germany, some 45 years after being taken there against my will as a captive of Soviet border troops.

returned to that reg putting my new sk an American-Russ My small detachm stioned officers ope border between th Hesse and Thuring representing Head Constabulary, loca through contact in liaison officers fror Guards Army, stati Among our duties incidents along the the return of AWC aircraft crews dove the Airlift Corridor

2LT Lincoln Landis '45, Russian Liaison Officer (Germany), 1947–48

d that Asbach in 1993 remem- "the incident of September " Indeed, villagers Erich Meder Georg Thomas, whom I chanced et, had been teenage witnesses to venit. A strange nostalgia swept me as they recounted precise and quickly led me to that ar site—the meadow alongside ountry road near—Asbach, d meters inside the old American

felt like I had discovered old s from an earlier day—these gers who recalled watching a officer lead his soldiers across

Title excerpt of author's article "The Village of Asbach Remembers," West Point alumni magazine *Assembly* July/August 1996.

know the numbers, and they are shestsot pyatdecat devyat (659) or pyatsot devyatnadsat (519).

I expected the captain to ignore these telephone numbers, but to my surprise, the Russian officer with a look of displeasure turned to his phone and made a call. After a few words to the other party on the line, he handed me the phone. It was Major Sazanov, who asked: "What the hell are you doing there?" I replied: "Don't ask me. Your folks arrested Morosky and me inside the American Zone where we were doing our duty. And, by the way, I'm not going to be able to meet you at our planned meeting at Wartha today."

Major Sazanov quickly replied: "Give the phone back to the captain." I did so and heard the captain say several times in a military tone of voice: "Slushayu, slushayu" (Yes Sir, Yes Sir). He hung up the phone, turned to me and said: "You are free to go."

Now that we Americans in captivity seemed to be gaining an advantage over our captors, I decided to become uncooperative, sensing that it was within the realm of liaising to try "payback time," and replied: "No, we are not going to go back now because it is time for lunch in the American Army, and we are hungry."

Again, the captain went negative, saying that it would not be possible to arrange lunch because it was too early for the Red Army to have its midday meal. I countered that the incident had been the fault of the Russians, and that we were hungry and wanted to eat. The captain shrugged, somewhat akin to Captain Morosov's earlier sheepishness when told that he would have to pay for a damaged American jeep, and, in a moment of some embarrassment, signaled: "Come on over here."

He led Morosky and me into his office, adorned with a familiar green-felt tablecloth and invited "his guests" to be seated. In a few minutes, a Russian soldier appeared in a rumpled, white uniform, bringing two bowls of meat-and-potato soup. The captain leaned casually against a wall and watched us devour the soup. The soldier in whites appeared again, took away the soup bowls, and served two plates with meat and potatoes that, while reminiscent of the soup, were much appreciated by the captive Americans.

As time passed, I began, with Morosky's assistance at translation, telling the captain a number of x-rated Red Army jokes that I had learned in language training. The captain found them most amusing, and, as he slouched more comfortably against the wall, proceeded to laugh uproariously at each tasteless joke. We savored the moment -- the captives were captivating their captor. *The captain was frank and friendly, and communist authority was unraveling.*

After finishing their lunch, I thanked the captain for his hospitality and said we were ready to depart, but on one condition -- that the two West German border police, complete with their pistols, were to be on hand for release as well. The captain gave a reluctant nod to this request. Then he gave me a choice: "How do you want to go back -- by way of Asbach, or by this better and shorter route directly to the border?"

I wanted very much for the villagers of Asbach to observe that we Americans had not been sent to Siberia but had been released un-harmed by the Russians, and told the captain: "back to Asbach." It soon became clear that the return trip was not through Asbach but was by his other selected route. The captain had acted precisely in opposition to the scenario that would enable the villagers to see that the Russians were forced to return the U.S. Army captives to the American Zone.

Upon arriving at the zonal border, the captain, with a bit of ceremony, stated his regret about the incident and wished our liaison team well. Then, he asked if we Americans had anything we wished to say. Feeling frustrated in not having the opportunity to let the Asbachers see that the Russians, in this case, did not liquidate their captives, I had nothing to say.

Sergeant Morosky, however, who, like me, had been thoroughly enjoying the many memorable aspects as "prisoners of the Cold War," had a different idea. With a sense of the captain's "funny bone," Pete declared, with contrived seriousness: "Tak. Ya sovietsky dezertir." (Yes, I am a Soviet deserter.") The captain, momentarily taken aback, quickly recovered, perhaps by recalling the levity that prevailed at lunchtime in his office, and smiled, slapping Morosky on the shoulder, and saying: "Sookin sin!" (in Russian "sonuvabitch" with the jovial meaning of "devilish rascal.")

Other Soviet officers standing nearby, however, were stunned by "Morosky's confession" and seemed quite ready to take drastic action against him, until they saw that their captain was enjoying the charade. While I admit that I had also been momentarily unnerved by my sergeant's joke, I gave Pete credit for knowing the Russians inside and out. Then we headed back in the American zone in our jeep. Again, *the captain was frank and friendly, and communist ideology was unraveling.*

We had apparently taken "liaising" to the limit. This Asbach incident had started with me and Morosky being captured in the American Zone and marched by the Red Army patrol "prisoner style" into the Russian Zone. Quickly, the episode seemed to launch the unraveling of Soviet authority thanks to a series of diffident responses by Soviet officers involved. Initial hostility yielded to accommodation time and again that led to an atmosphere of good humor and even an apology. *Soviet authority had crumbled, and friendliness took its place.* Lessons had been learned: Direct action at the grass roots, not formal negotiations between American and Soviet officials, had borne fruit. The Asbach incident provided good evidence that, as far as military personnel of the lower ranks were concerned, the so-called "Cold War" was an irrelevant distraction.

To bring this account to a full conclusion, the calendar must be moved forward a period of 45 years. My long-held ambition to "get the word back to Asbachers" that the Russians had not liquidated the Americans and Germans on that memorable day had not been possible until the end of the Cold War. Finally, in 1993, now a retired lieutenant colonel, I found an opportunity, after the Soviet Union's collapse and withdrawal of military forces from East

Germany, to return to the site of the illegal seizure of my team with the two U.S.-German border policemen.

With my wife Donna and son Timothy, I flew to Frankfurt, Germany and drove directly to that border area and the village of Asbach, hoping to make a belated appearance to achieve my goal. My first step was to find a resident who might have witnessed "the event of August 1948." I knocked on many doors to no avail until one villager provided the address of a certain resident who had indeed lived, he claimed, in the village during the Berlin Airlift. This was an encouraging sign, but I wondered if the individual would recall, or wish to discuss, the actions of Soviet forces against the liaison team.

After arriving at the appropriate house, I inquired whether the resident, one Erich Meder, had witnessed the incident in which Russian troops had entered the American Zone and captured a US Army lieutenant and sergeant and two German border police. Herr Meder replied that he did recall very clearly how the Red Army patrol marched the Americans into Asbach and took them away to the East.

I introduced myself as "that lieutenant" and, to verify Meder's account, asked him to walk through the village and indicate the spot in the meadow where the capture had taken place. The Asbacher confirmed the accuracy of his recollection by walking to the edge of the village and pointing to the site of the event. At last, I was convinced that I had "gotten the word back" that the Russians were compelled to allow the American and German captives to return unharmed to the American Zone.

When the "former lieutenant" explained that he did not understand why the Russians acted as they did against the Americans, Meder replied that the Russian captain was very concerned because on the previous day, some Americans were hunting wild boar and firing their guns. His explanation finally satisfied my long-held curiosity about the nature of Soviet motivations to take us as prisoners in the American zone during the Berlin Airlift in August 1948.

I then asked Meder if there happened to be any other Asbacher who would have witnessed the arrest, and Meder proceeded to call to an upstairs window of a nearby dwelling. I recognized the building as the old Soviet headquarters where Morosky and I had been questioned. In response, Meder's friend Georg Thomas came down, and the three, Meder, Thomas and I posed for a picture to commemorate the final chapter in the incident that happened so many years ago. The important moment was recorded on film when Donna photographed me, standing in the middle, arm-in-arm with Erich and Georg. Somehow, this was a reminder of an earlier time, when "liaising" had led to another get-together, helping the Russians -- Major Kris and Lieutenant Volkov -- to celebrate the 30th anniversary of the Bolshevik Revolution.

Upon our return to the United States, I managed to contact Sergeant Morosky, and we relived this event with great joy during a long telephone conversation. Pete was now in ill health, and his few remaining years did not permit a face-to-face reunion. We would have had many laughs in recalling the good times we shared including the short captivity as possibly Russia's only "American Army prisoners of the Cold War," who managed to talk their way into being released. A typical diplomatic solution would have been complex and possibly not as favorable.

It had been a busy August 1948, not only for the pilots who were flying day-and-night in the Frankfurt-to-Tempelhof Berlin Airlift corridor, but also for the liaison team on the ground below. One episode even made stateside newspapers after Constabulary Headquarters informed the team that one of our Berlin Airlift planes had gone down in the Russian Zone, and the fate of the pilots was not known.

I had been directed to call a meeting with Colonel Garber and Major Sazanov, who continued to travel in pairs, to inform them of the aborted Airlift flight. I met with them, providing the bare facts of the C-47 aircraft incident and requesting their assistance in returning the pilots to the American side. The Soviet team showed great interest and asked for detailed information to include the name and description of the pilots. I did not have this information but would not have provided it to the Russians anyway because of the rare chance that the pilots might evade arrest and find safe haven in the Russian zone.

I also sensed that Garber and Sazanov were quite aware of the aircraft's fate and were eager to find out as much as possible in order to be able to apprehend the pilots. At this stage in American-Russian relations, it was not clear as to the kind of treatment the Red Army had in mind for American pilots that might be downed while flying in the Berlin Airlift corridors. (U.S. Air Force pre-flight briefings were reported to have included a dire warning, apparently based upon a garbled version of my failure to be officially returned after disappearing via Red Army Captain Morosov's patrol that seized me and Morosky in the in the American Zone near the Thuringian border a few weeks earlier.)

At midnight, the U.S. German border post contacted me by phone, reporting that a man claiming to be a Berlin Airlift pilot had clandestinely arrived from the Russian Zone. I went out immediately and took into custody U.S. Air Force Captain Kenneth Slaker. I also learned about the East German who had risked his own life to bring Slaker to the American Zone.

The pair had come across at an illegal crossing point around midnight and survived a hail of bullets from Soviet border guards. The U.S.-West German border police processed Slaker's East German guide as a refugee in order to keep his identity from being made known to Soviet and East German authority. It was clear that he and his family would be treated severely for protecting an American pilot who had bailed out over East Germany.

I returned Captain Slaker, who was tired but in good condition, to the town of Hersfeld, where he was evacuated to higher Air Force headquarters. In the meantime, Slaker related to me his experience after bailing out of his C-47 aircraft. He had landed in a potato field, rolled up his chute in the dead of night, proceeded to a nearby road and began walking in hopes of finding his way back to the American Zone. He did not know where he was headed, but suddenly found good fortune.

While walking along a country road, he had struck up a conversation with an East German worker with pro-American feelings based on the humane way in which he had been treated as a German prisoner of war in the United States. Consequently, the East German chose to help this downed Berlin Airlift pilot in an effort to get him back safely into the American Zone. As a first step he made sure that Captain Slaker turned his American flight jacket inside out to avoid detection.

The captain continued his narrative, noting that he and the East German boarded a train, where Slaker's self-appointed guide handed the pilot an apple to be held in front of his face in order to screen his American identity. The pair arrived at the German's home, where the guide fashioned a plan for getting Slaker back into the American Zone. It was to be carried out under cover of darkness the same evening in order to avoid being discovered by Russian or German security guards.

In this process, he worked out a detailed route in the direction of the border that included, for example, bribing a certain bridge guard at a particular hour in the evening. Later, that night, the resourceful and innovative guide hustled Captain Slaker past a number of curious onlookers that included suspicious Red Army officers enroute to the heavily-guarded border region.

At a precise moment, the East German guide gave Slaker the signal to make the dash forward together with a group of illegal border-crossers, seeking to avoid detection by East German and Soviet border guards. The group succeeded in reaching the American side in the dark of night under a hail of Russian rifle fire.

The next day, I returned to a meeting with Colonel Garber and Major Sazanov and again requested their assistance in finding and returning the pilots, "whose names were still unknown." It would not have been prudent to have "leveled" with the Russians about Slaker's return because Garber and Sazanov might have been able to assist in the process of tracking down and exposing the East Germans who had risked their lives to return Slaker to freedom.

Furthermore, the liaison team had no information about the whereabouts of the other pilot. The U.S. side continued to hold out hope that he would be able to evade Russian troops and find refuge among friendly East Germans or return safely to American custody. This was a sensitive moment when I realized that "good liaising" would mean deceiving my Soviet counterparts, who were obviously frustrated by their inability to locate the downed pilots. As it happened, the other pilot was apprehended by Red Army authorities, who, fortunately, elected to turn him over in good condition to American liaison personnel in West Berlin. In the case of Slaker, the Russians belatedly found out about his escape from the newspapers.

Again, turning the calendar forward 50 years, I was able to contact Kenneth Slaker and to learn that he had been treated as a hero by Berliners who honored him at the 50th Anniversary of the Airlift, celebrated in the city in 1998. The local German press described Slaker as "the angel who crashed in the Zone." His description as "the angel" emanated from the pilot's own characterization of his personal feelings, flying aircraft loaded with coal or flour to Tempelhof Airbase for people in need in West Berlin.

Early signs appeared 60 years ago, in 1948, when the KGB (then NKVD) went wishy-washy in releasing two American detainees in Occupied Germany. On this occasion when American planes were flying the Airlift in this corridor, my team's liaison activities received rare exposure to the wider world. I was negotiating with Garber and Sazanov concerning the Russian apprehension of two American officials along the zonal border. According to one article in the *New York Times* "Two Held by Soviet Asked to Admit Guilt," I had found the men "clean and in good condition" when the Russians arrived at the border to turn them over some five days after they had been arrested.

The Soviet side insisted that I acknowledge in a signed receipt that the wayward officials were guilty of entering the Russian Zone and taking illegal pictures. I refused to sign such a receipt after explaining that the Americans were not guilty of violating the border and wrongfully using a camera. The article of August 20 added "the American lieutenant remained adamant" after the Russians tried "sometimes in a friendly manner and sometimes in a rough manner" to persuade the liaison officer to sign such a receipt. In a follow-up article "Freed Officials Tired of Cabbage," the newspaper reported on August 23, that, after 18 days, "the men were released today to Lieutenant Lincoln Landis who said he had signed a simple receipt."

After at first refusing to accept custody of these wayward officials, I recall being compelled to make it clear to the Soviet side that the Americans were not guilty of taking illegal pictures nor of violating the border. The NKVD officers, charged with border security, quickly became conciliatory and agreed to turn over the detainees as simply "two persons." This pattern of Russian attitudes -- hostile-turned-cooperative, and off-times friendly -- became an established feature of encounters with Russian representatives, both military and civilian, throughout much of the Cold War. *It became obvious to me: communist authority was unraveling.*

Having experienced up front this early period of a congenial war aka Cold War 1947-1948, I turned down an opportunity to be re-assigned as an instructor of the Russian language at West Point. Instead, my next liaison work with the Russians would include intensive training, again at Oberammergau Germany. My following assignment then placed me in the U.S. Military Liaison Mission at Potsdam, a suburb of Berlin in 1961.

III. Unraveling during the Berlin Wall crisis 1961-1963

As a graduation gesture for completing a four-year program in the Russian Foreign Area Specialist Program, students including now-Major Landis were on their way to the Soviet Union in April 1961. First, however, the trip from Germany came to a temporary halt in Vienna because of a disastrous bit of timing: the U.S. invasion of Cuba was not a good moment for dispatching a group of Russian Area specialists into the U.S.S.R.

After President Kennedy called off the invasion, however, the picture brightened, and higher authority gave the go-ahead for the train trip to Kiev. Once in a hotel in that capital of Ukraine, "we tourists" found an opportunity to wander in the streets and engage local citizens in conversation.

I came upon a group that was admiring a shiny sedan near the hotel. When I heard the question: "Where did this car come from?" and an answer: "It must be from one of the democratic countries." This proved to be an opportunity to practice my Russian: "No, it is not from one of the democratic countries . . . it is an Opel, and it comes from West Germany." (Editorial note: "democratic countries" in Russian referred not to democratic countries of the West, but to the so-called "demokraticheskiye stranny," East European communist countries.)

The group was somewhat taken aback by the appearance of an outsider, whose clothing style probably looked like that of an American. My sudden participation in their discussion led them to respond nearly in unison: "Oh, that explains everything." They had expressed the view that, for quality goods as in the case of automobiles, one had to look abroad, perhaps to other communist countries but more likely to the capitalist West. As a final note, one of the groups embarrassed the others standing nearby by asking me if he could buy my shoes. Another of the group spoke out, reproaching his friend with: "What would he (Landis) wear?"

They were frank and friendly and showed unraveling about the scarce availability of items in the Soviet Union compared with East European communist countries or the United States.

In July 1961, I took my new assignment with the U. S. Military Liaison Mission at Potsdam, located in East Germany as a suburb of Berlin. The change from the "Russian Zone" to "East Germany" ("the German Democratic Republic") occurred as the Soviet response to U.S. tutelage of the American Zone to be known as "West Germany" ("the Federal Republic of Germany.") My first duty in U.S.M.L.M. was as "tour officer," one of a group of officers, who, with an American soldier as driver, would travel through Soviet-occupied East Germany.

The work of the U.S. military liaison team of 1961 differed markedly from that of my earlier Russian liaison team, vintage Berlin Airlift of 1948, who merely "liaised" on the zonal border. The Potsdam team's area of operation was the Soviet-occupied country of East Germany, with the exception of "restricted areas," where Soviet or East German military facilities were located.

The U.S. military liaison team had been created, along with British and French teams that would also travel through East Germany as a provision of the Potsdam Agreement of 1945 signed by President Truman, Prime Minister Winston Churchill, and Premier Stalin. In exchange, the Russians fielded their own "Potsdam Mission teams" in the American, British and French occupied zones of West Germany.

The Soviet liaison teams also were free to travel without escort like the Western teams and were similarly restricted from entering maneuver areas and military installations.

On the night of August 12, 1961, just a month after I had started my new assignment at Potsdam, I received a memorable phone call at midnight. The voice was that of Captain Leo Geleta, U.S. Air Force member of U.S.M.L.M. on duty at the West Berlin Office, who spoke carefully in urgent terms: "You must come down to the office immediately."

I dressed quickly and drove to the office where I was met by Geleta standing at the front door, declaring: "This is it!" I questioned him about the meaning of "it," and Geleta replied in an earnest voice: "The balloon is up, World War III!"

Leo went on to explain that he and Major Dave Morgan, another tour officer, had just returned from Krampnitz, where they barely avoided onrushing Soviet tanks. He explained that when he and Dave passed the gates of the kaserne housing the Soviet 10th Guards Tank Division, all was quiet, but within a few minutes upon their return, the gates opened, and out came the tanks. Leo and Dave had to hustle in their 1961 Ford Fairlane, with interceptor engine, to keep ahead of the tanks.

There was an uproar at the West Berlin Headquarters of the United States Military Liaison Mission to the Group of Soviet Forces Germany. It soon became known that East Germans were constructing a barrier near the U.S. border post "Checkpoint Charlie." West Berliners, who were mindful of American support when they were beleaguered until America and Britain came to their aid in 1948 via the Berlin Airlift, now were again concerned. They were hopeful that the United States and Britain would reinforce their garrisons in the face of the growing threat from the Soviet Union, East Germany's benefactor.

For four days they waited for a sign of American resolve. Finally, on the fifth day, they had reason for celebration as the United States moved a military unit from the British zonal check point at Helmstedt. By chance, it fell to me, one of the newest members of the Potsdam Mission, to head west out of West Berlin in a mission car to meet up with the American convoy of jeeps and trucks moving along the autobahn from Helmstedt. Upon meeting the convoy, *Major Linc Landis, freshly assigned to the Potsdam Mission, had the good fortune to lead it to reinforce the U.S. military garrison in West Berlin!*

When the convoy came into view, my driver did a U-turn on the autobahn, crossing the grassy strip, and led the troops through the Soviet check point into West Berlin. The troops were very tired because they had been waiting for President Kennedy's decision that finally went into effect on Thursday, August 17th. West Berliners were ecstatic. Their worries about the possibility of being taken over by superior Soviet forces that had surrounded the city were abated, at least for the time being.

What gratitude I felt for the opportunity to be a part of the process to demonstrate to West Berliners and the world that the West would again take a firm stand on the side of freedom! The moment was also electrifying for the American, British and French garrisons in the city. The pride was everywhere in the isolated city. History was being made again: In 1948, the Western Allies had met Stalin's challenge. In 1961, the United States led the way to meet Khrushchev's ploy.

There was the possibility that Nikita Khrushchev had underestimated President Kennedy at their meeting several months earlier in Vienna, so quickly after JFK's inauguration. At any rate, the Soviet premier's decision to send World War II hero, Marshal Konev, to take charge of the Group of Soviet Forces Germany around the 1st of August seemed to have been no coincidence.

The East German action to erect barricades in the heart of Germany's historic capital was considered by many as a signal to the West that the Cold War might begin to replace the congeniality that my liaison functions had experienced to date. At this time, Jack Parr's television show at Checkpoint Charlie in West Berlin was providing daily coverage of the "U.S.-Soviet confrontation" of tanks, "nose-to-nose" while East Germans proceeded to construct a barrier in the heart of the city. This program carried "live" around the world conveying the message that "the Cold War" was heating up.

Authoritative thinking about these developments seemed to indicate that construction of a barrier between East and West Berlin was a pragmatic and "necessary" last-ditch measure by East Germany. It was intended to staunch the flow of professional employees to the West via the porous

Berlin border region. Although the U.S.S.R. was giving full support to the East German plan, there was no apparent evidence of a Soviet effort to raise the stakes of confrontation with the Western powers.

As for the Western military liaison presence in East Germany, the American, British, and French liaison teams now had intensified reason to look out for Western interests. For the Soviet military liaison missions (called "Soxmis"), they too could be counted upon to be active in daily excursions through the American, British, and French portions of West Germany.

As a tour officer, I was mindful of my previous experience working along the American and Russian zonal borders during the Berlin Airlift in 1948. At that time, I entered the Russian Zone only to represent U.S. Constabulary Headquarters in Heidelberg with my Russian opposite numbers from the Headquarters of the Eighth Guards Army in Weimar, East Germany. Now, as a Potsdam Mission officer, I needed to become familiar with cities and the countryside of East Germany in order to avoid undesirable confrontations with Soviet military authorities.

In my previous assignment, I had the opportunity to interact openly with my counterparts, Colonel Garber and Major Sazanov, as well as "my friend" in charge of the Soviet border post at Wartha, Major Kris, before he was apparently cashiered. Now, in 1961, such "grassroots" contact along the borders between the U.S. - occupied States of Hesse and Bavaria, respectively, and the Russian-occupied States of Thuringia and Saxony was no longer possible.

The new situation had emerged in 1952, when East Germany under Soviet direction constructed a physical barrier with watch towers, ploughed strips, electrified fences, guard dogs and a 24-hour military presence along the entire border from the English Channel to Czechoslovakia. As a result, liaison contact regarding military issues arising in East Germany between U.S. and the U.S.S.R. elements rose to the level of the chief of the U.S. mission at Potsdam in negotiation with a "Potsdam" representative of the Group of Soviet Forces Germany at Wunsdorf.

With the U.S. Military Liaison Mission, contact between us "touring officers" and Soviet military forces in the field was to be avoided, although inadvertent contact did occur. The entire concept of this type of liaison organization was to provide confidence-building measures that would serve the interest of peaceful relations between the United States, Britain and France, on the one hand, and the Soviet Union, on the other.

One anecdote that resulted from inadvertent contact with Soviet military units took place on a road that led to an area where Soviet military exercises apparently were taking place. My official car, with its American Mission status clearly displayed, was halted by a Soviet sentry who stated that the Potsdam Mission car could not proceed further and would be required to turn around and depart the scene. It seemed to be a moment to test whether congenial liaison relations would still be in effect during the Berlin Wall crisis as was evident during the Berlin Airlift crisis a dozen or so years earlier.

I chose to try to advance the principle of freedom of movement in areas that were not permanently restricted, which would cause Soviet armed guards to summon higher authority to the scene. The sentry, with his tommy gun at port arms, stood in the middle of the road and informed me in Russian that my vehicle would have to remain in place until his lieutenant would arrive to resolve the situation.

In order to pass the time and test the sentry, I got out of my Mission vehicle and started to shave with a battery razor near the front of the vehicle in plain view of the guard. (Such shavers, in the timeframe of 1961, were commonplace in the United States, but, apparently, were unknown to soldiers of Soviet Forces in Germany and perhaps in the Soviet Union as well.) Not surprisingly, the Soviet guard expressed an immediate interest in "what the major was up to" and approached closely to satisfy his curiosity. I told him, in

Russian, that it was a battery shaver, and I handed it to him, saying: "Here, give it a try."

Reluctant, at first, to comply, the sentry thought about his job of guarding against American intrusion into Soviet military operations, particularly now in the crisis atmosphere of the Berlin Wall. The road guard also had to consider that his fellow Red Army soldiers were watching him nearby from the ditch of the road. Then, he made his decision, shifted his machine gun from the ready position with which he was guarding me and my driver, and slung it from his shoulder so that it was pointing up in the air. He carefully took hold of my razor and proceeded to shave his face.

This sentry's joyful abandonment of his military responsibility, coupled with his strong satisfaction from the shaving experience, proved too much for his fellow soldiers in the ditch. They thoroughly enjoyed his caper, while also being concerned about what their lieutenant would think upon his arrival. Apparently, the sentry also began to sense a possible predicament and, with a big grin, handed the shaver back to me.

Upon his lieutenant's arrival, the sentry had quickly resumed his proper guard position with his gun at the ready, returning us to his military control. His fellow soldiers quickly controlled the glee they had shown during the shaving event. The Soviet officer issued the standard warning to me that the U.S. mission was in violation and was required to turn around and exit the area. Of course, the lieutenant was on solid ground in doing his duty properly, and my driver and I departed.

To me, this episode was most gratifying because it reinforced my previous observations that Soviet military personnel might, even under risky circumstances, discard their vigilant opposition and embrace a friendly American initiative. *This guard had set aside his security duty in order to show congeniality to the American,* who had deliberately tested the limits of the sentry's rigid military regulations. To the road guard and his colleagues laughing in the ditch, this "threatening American" wasn't really a threat after all. In fact, he had acted like a friend, and the Russian responded in kind. *These Red Army soldiers displayed their sense of duty was unraveling even during the tension caused by the Wall crisis.*

This guard's reaction fitted my conclusions about "the Soviet mind" because it resembled a split personality. Thus, on many occasions, Russians had demonstrated an underlying readiness to accept American friendship in the face of communist proscriptions. For example, this sentry and his fellow soldiers showed no indication that tension between the U.S. and Soviet military forces had risen as a result of the crisis surrounding Soviet-sponsored East German actions to divide the city of Berlin.

On another liaison trip, with another Mission officer on board, we deliberately traveled "too close" to a Red Army camp in order to detect their unit designation, resulting in another Soviet detention in the central region of East Germany. We Americans were led into the office of the Soviet colonel in charge of the military region, and, from behind his familiar, green-felt-covered desk, he issued in a routine manner a standard "violation" warning. The colonel remained relaxed, showing no sense of irritation.

After a few minutes, I requested and obtained his permission to use the restroom down the hallway. While there, I observed what seemed to be standard practice in the use of the official communist newspaper as toilet paper. I raised the issue with the colonel by stating that there appeared to be no toilet paper in the bathroom, and the colonel disagreed, saying that there were plenty of Russian newspapers on the hook. The colonel did not specify whether he read the official press organ of the Communist Party of the Soviet Union "Pravda" before it arrived on the toilet hook.

Here again, although the liaison team had been seen to be in obvious, confrontational violation, the senior Soviet officer-in-charge carried out his duty in an agreeable manner. The encounter with the colonel was amicable from start to finish. It was evident that this senior military officer "in the field" showed no major concern about us (who had been in obvious violation) and *was frank and friendly. His dedication to military readiness appeared to be tentative, and his lack of commitment to communist authority was on display.*

A non-military event that related to President Kennedy's visit to Berlin concerned Pat Lawford and Jean Smith, the President's sisters. I encountered them one Sunday morning when I was visiting my Potsdam Mission office and discovered they had lost their way while wandering alone about the neighborhood in West Berlin. Fortunately, I was able to deliver them safely to Ambassador Dowling's quarters, where they had been staying.

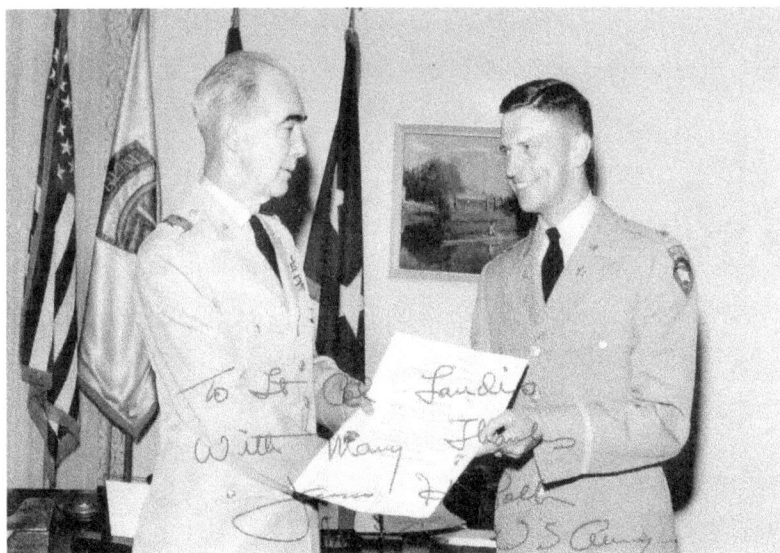

Commander of Berlin Command, General James Polk, gives "Guardian of Berlin" award to Lieutenant Colonel Lincoln Landis upon completion of his US Military Liaison Mission assignment, 1963.

IV. Unraveling during détente 1976-1977

Now retired after 20 years of "active duty," mostly in Russian Area assignments, I continued with one-on-one opportunities to become familiar with "the unraveling" in the mid-1970s. My current duty was as civilian adviser to the White House on U.S.-U.S.S.R. cooperation during the period of détente. The scope of my assignment was to evaluate the exchange agreements signed by President Richard Nixon and General Secretary of the Communist Party of the Soviet Union Leonid Brezhnev in 1972. The major fields of cooperation included research in: Science and Technology, Space, Transportation, Energy, Environment, Public Health, and Artificial Heart, and it was time for President Ford to decide whether to renew them for another five years.

I attended sessions of the Joint Working Group on Science Policy that held week-long meetings in Washington, D.C. in the mid-1970s. Both sides concerned themselves with similarities and differences in the two nations' approach to research procedures and productivity matters.

The twin panels were headed by an American director of a leading civilian academic organization and senior Soviet officials representing areas of science and technology. I listened to individual discussions by the U.S. Working Group that included specialists in economics and representatives of industry along with members of the Soviet Working Group. The latter included high government officials including national directors for Science and Technology and the State Planning Committee. Russian and English language interpreters facilitated the exchange of views during the daily sessions.

The meetings provided spirited exchanges consisting of charges made by the Soviet chairman that cited "examples of deficiencies in capitalist methods" in contrast with "superior practices in the Soviet system." One example focused upon an article published in Forbes Magazine that acknowledged only a small percentage of basic research performed in American institutions was expected to lead to large-scale production. This would constitute "unacceptable waste" in the U.S.S.R., the Soviet chairman claimed and would not be tolerated in Soviet industry.

In this case, the American side offered further explanation indicating that basic research in the United States frequently led to advanced research before the results are made available to industrial production. Instead of being considered wasteful, such basic research is merely one essential element in a chain of U.S. research practices that assure more efficiency than if production began after basic research alone. Little consensus could be reached after lively discussions, especially through reservations or opposition by the Soviet side.

Following five days of serious arguments presented by both sides, the working groups found the sessions to have been "informative and productive" for both sides. At the close of the final session, the Soviet chairman requested that I serve as a guide and interpreter in accompanying his working group on a shopping trip to "Tyson Corner," established during previous exchange visits as a popular Russian destination. I agreed to accept this opportunity and met with the group the following day to escort the chairman and his associates to "Tyson Corner."

Upon meeting the group, I recognized a high-level of excitement among all members of the Soviet Working Group. Replacing the dour business attitudes displayed during the week was a new high level of anticipation on the part of these keenly-motivated individuals, including their KGB member. They had promptly assembled in front of their low-grade hotel which, I had already understood, was standard practice for previously-visiting Soviet officials. (These groups consistently chose inexpensive, and somewhat questionable hotels in order to save maximum dollars to spend in the department stores.)

Interest level was at a peak, and it became clear that this weekend activity promised to be the highlight of the Russians' visits to the United States during "détente." No mention was made of matters dealt with during the earlier business sessions. All attention was directed toward arrival at "Tyson Corner." One of the senior members of the Soviet delegation made a special request to be able to go to "Heks bergen bessment," a newly-minted Russian term for a prominent store at Tyson's Corner.

The excitement continued upon entering Hechts Bargain Basement, and the Soviet official instructed me that he wished to acquire a T-shirt for his wife. At the display of T-shirts, he chose one that featured a large picture of the Parthenon, and when the clerk, a stoutly-built lady, arrived to consummate the purchase, she asked the Soviet visitor "who are you buying this T-shirt for?" When the official responded: "for my wife who is built like you," the clerk protested: "Oh, no! Do not buy her this picture of the Parthenon . . . I would never wear it." The visitor was adamant in choosing the T-shirt and asked about the cost. When the dismayed clerk responded: "$1.75," the visitor paid, adding: "We have them in the Soviet Union, and they are much better and cheaper, but I'll take it."

Meanwhile, the chairman of the group arrived at another department store and asked me to select a jacket for his grandson. I selected one, and the chairman replied: "I'll take it." When I stated (with an attempt at humor): "You may not want this because it was made in capitalist Korea," the senior official replied: "Stop pulling my leg. You know that's just what I came for. I'll take it."

I concluded my role as a guide to the Soviet officials with a distinct impression that these senior officials, members of the Communist Party, exhibited the same attitudes that many years earlier, in the years of the Berlin Airlift crisis of 1948, and the Berlin Wall crisis of 1961, closely resembled the attitudes of Red Army personnel: Attitudes of restraint and antagonism dissolved, turning to *a frank unraveling of regard for the Soviet Union's communist system.*

The unraveling seemed to continue unabated, whether Russian citizens involved were soldiers, military officers, or now, high and middle-level government and Party bureaucrats

– all quite ready to express their strong preferences for American goods and the capitalistic system of government.

While American Kremlinologists and intelligence officials remained uniform in declaring that the Soviet system's great vulnerability was its "inefficient and wasteful economy," little if any attention was given to the decisive rejection by ordinary citizens and party officials themselves of the day-to-day workings of the Soviet system. They remained oblivious, in my view, to the strong likelihood that the basic vulnerability was the unraveling of communism in the U.S.S.R. from Day One of the Cold War.

V. "Collapse" revealed in a grassroots revolution!

As I have indicated in previous pages, Washington's utter failure to understand the previous Cold War's demise has rested upon a nebulous concept of "collapse." So much for the long-favored theory that only a "Soviet economic collapse" would "bring the U.S.S.R. to its knees." Surprising to our Kremlinologists, that kind of collapse failed to occur.

The astonishing end of "the Cold War" proved that the Western world was unversed in Russia's "collapse" as shown in the previously mentioned statement of the Librarian of Congress described to the American Academy of Arts and Sciences as an unexpected, unexplainable, "great historical drama" . . . lacking a name. His update after 20 years to Russia House was an "implosion of the Soviet system . . . totally unanticipated, and we still don't understand it."

My liaison assignments, however, produced for me a congenial dimension of "the Cold War" at the local level. These one-on-one experiences brought me in touch with officials representing the Soviet High Command in Occupied Germany during the Berlin Airlift crisis in 1948 and the Berlin Wall crisis in 1961. Similarly, in the mid-1970s, I dealt with U.S.-U.S.S.R. cooperative working-groups during détente as a White House adviser.

Acrimony shown by the U.S.S.R.'s leadership during the so-called "Cold War" was, in my view, out-of-step with pro-American sentiments of various segments of Soviet society. I have concluded that a terminal condition of governance in the Soviet Union existed from Day One of the U.S.S.R.'s membership in the United Nations in 1945.

From the early days of the post-World War II period, communist authority unraveled, I believe, through the Berlin Airlift crisis of 1948 and the Berlin Wall crisis of 1961. Furthermore, during the détente period including President Ford's decision in 1976 to renew bilateral détente programs,

Russians continued to display positive attitudes toward this U.S. liaison official and for American products. I found evidence of a remarkable and consistent pattern of pro-American and anti-regime attitudes. This strongly suggested to me that Muscovites, observing Party rule to be in disarray, went to the streets in August 1991, proceeding to seize the first opportunity to make their case for freedom. Unarmed and without apparent leadership, they gathered in Moscow and carried out, I believe, a popular, spontaneous, peaceable, pro-American and anti-regime revolution. Misunderstood by Kremlinologists, I conclude, this sudden turn of events persuaded Party maverick, Federation President Boris Yeltsin, to proclaim the end of communism in Russia.

If a Russian grassroots revolution of August 1991 had enjoyed the legitimacy I believe it fully deserved, one might envision at least two intriguing policy outcomes:

■ Would a decision in the West to maintain the North Atlantic Treaty Organization have been affected?

■ If not, would NATO plans for eastward expansion have garnered decisive support?

Earlier Writings

Books

Politics and Oil: Moscow in the Middle East; Dunellen Press, 1973.

Gorbachev's Hidden Agenda – Glimpses of the Soviet Mind; Vantage Press, 1991.

From Pilgrimage to Promise, Civil War Heritage and the Landis Boys of Logansport, Indiana; Heritage Books, Inc. 2006.

Articles

"Middle East Crises and the USSR" *World Affairs*, April, May, June 1967.

"Soviet Interest in Middle East Oil" *The New Middle East* No. 3, London EC4, 1968.

"Der Suezkanal in der politschen Strategie der Sowjetunion" *EUROPA ARCHIV*, Bonn, Germany, February 10, 1969.

"Soviet Perceptions, Soviet Motives" *Studies in Third World Societies*, Department of Anthropology, College of William and Mary, 1981.

"Motives and Perceptions in the USSR's Global Outreach" *What Lies Ahead?* US Air Force, U.S.Government Printing Office 1982.

"Landis Explores the Old and the New Soviet Mind" *Miller Center Report*, University of Virginia; Summer, 1992.

"Prisoners of the Cold War – The Village of Asbach Remembers" *ASSEMBLY*, United States Military Academy, July/August, 1996.

ABOUT THE AUTHOR

I am optimistic that this book makes a timely appearance. If we would welcome a halt in the present drift toward a new Cold War—ordinary Russians cleared the way, I believe, for a new, constructive relationship by clobbering communism in August 1991.